OPTICAL
ILLUSIONS

EYE
TEASERS

Gareth Stevens
PUBLISHING

ANNA CLAYBOURNE

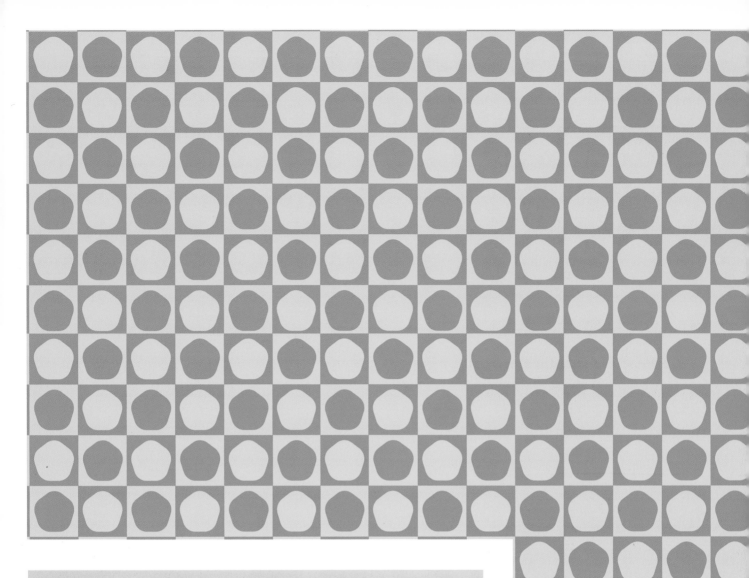

Please visit our website, **www.garethstevens.com**.
For a free color catalog of all our high-quality books,
call toll free 1-800-542-2595 or fax 1-877-542-2596.

Cataloging-in-Publication Data
Names: Claybourne, Anna.
Title: Eye teasers / Anna Claybourne.
Description: New York : Gareth Stevens Publishing, 2020. | Series: The science of optical
illusions | Includes glossary and index.
Identifiers: ISBN 9781538242414 (pbk.) | ISBN 9781538241851 (library bound) | ISBN
9781538242421 (6 pack)
Subjects: LCSH: Optical illusions--Juvenile literature. | Visual perception--Juvenile literature.
Classification: LCC QP495.C5725 2020 | DDC 152.14'8--dc23

First Edition

Published in 2020 by
Gareth Stevens Publishing
111 East 14th Street, Suite 349
New York, NY 10003

Photo credits: p16 r © Purves Lab; p17 t © Edward H. Adelson; p26 © Purves Lab;
p27 t © Fibonacci; p29 © Larry Kagan

Printed in the United States of America

CPSIA compliance information: Batch #CS19GS: For further information contact Gareth Stevens, New York, New York at
1-800-542-2595.

CONTENTS

INTRODUCTION

WHAT ARE OPTICAL ILLUSIONS?

The word "optical" has to do with light and how we see it. An illusion is something that tricks you, so that you don't experience it as it really is.

Magicians and illusionists make impossible things appear to happen. This performer can't really make this die levitate—but he makes it look as if he can.

SEEING IS BELIEVING

When we look around and see things, it feels to us as if we're simply seeing the world as it really is. However, that's not quite true. Your eyes and your brain can make mistakes, miss things, or even see things that aren't there. An optical illusion is a picture that takes advantage of these mistakes to play a trick on you.

HOW HUMANS SEE

1. Light rays from objects enter the eye.

2. Light hits the retina at the back of the eyeball.

3. Light-sensitive cells in the retina detect patterns of light.

4. The cells send signals to the brain along the optic nerve.

5. The brain interprets the signals to figure out what they mean.

Retina

Image on retina

Eyeball

Visual cortex

Optic nerve

Brain

4

TOO MUCH INFORMATION!

All day long, there's a constant flood of images entering your eyes and zooming into your brain. There's so much information, your brain simply can't process it all carefully.

Instead, it decides what it's looking at by matching the light patterns it sees to its memories and previous experiences. It ignores or shuts out things that don't seem important and will quickly jump to conclusions to save time.

Here's an example. What can you see in this picture? ▶

Most people would see two friends riding these. ▼

In other words, bicycles—machines with two round wheels of equal size. But you only "see" that because of your brain's knowledge and experience. The wheels you actually saw look like this:

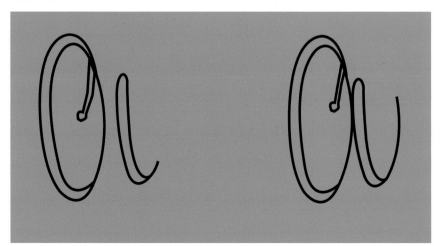

ILLUSIONS GALORE

This book is packed with incredible optical illusions to bamboozle your brain—from clever shadows to pictures that seem to change color.

Turn the page to get started!

LOOKING CROOKED

Straight or curved? That is the question!

Take a look at this tiled pattern, and answer the simple question: Are the narrow orange lines straight? They can't be! They look like they're all over the place and totally wonky. ▶

But—you guessed it—they actually are all straight and all perfectly parallel to each other. Don't believe it? Take a pencil, and line it up between them.

In fact, if you took away the bricks in between, the picture would look like this. ▼

How Does It Work?

It's the positioning of the tiles in a zigzag pattern that confuses the brain. We're more used to seeing simple checkerboard or brickwork patterns, in which darker and lighter areas are evenly balanced. In this pattern, the darker bricks run in zigzags. This makes the orange lines seem unbalanced and appear to lean toward each other.

That's Weird!

This is called the café wall illusion, since it was spotted on a real tiled café wall in Bristol, UK, in 1973. Imagine being the tiler who had to make the pattern … you'd constantly be thinking you'd done it wrong!

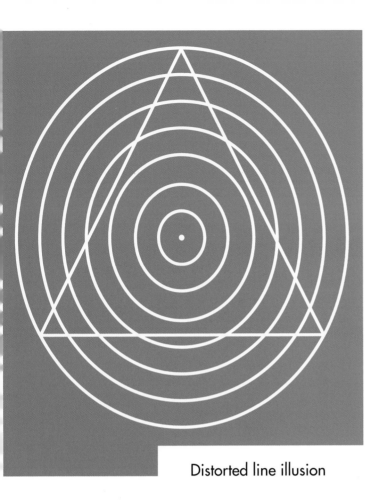

Distorted line illusion

THE SQUASHED TRIANGLE

In this illusion, a triangle sits on top of a bull's-eye of concentric circles—but try as you might, you can't see it as a normal triangle. It looks all squashed and pushed in. The lines around it make the triangle's sides seem to curve away from them, so they look bent.

Brain-Boggling!

It's actually really hard for your brain to simply see things on their own. It's always comparing lines and shapes to what's around them. This helps the brain decide what it's looking at.

BEND IT LIKE HERING!

This is one of the simplest crooked-looking illusions of them all—the Hering illusion. A spoke-like background makes the red lines look bent, but of course, they're not! (Test them with a ruler.) Though it seems so simple, scientists haven't yet been able to agree on exactly how it works.

To make your own illusion, trace the black lines, then try adding different shapes, such as a square or circle, on top. What happens to them?

Hering illusion

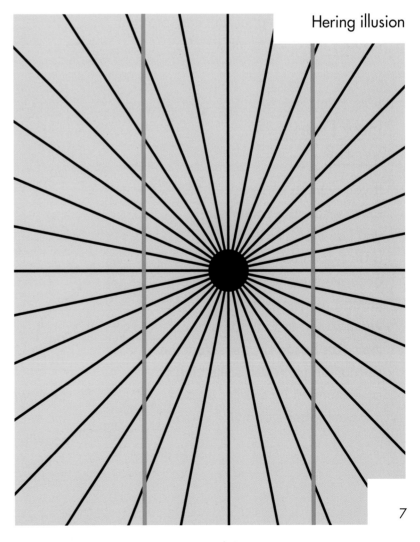

BIGGER OR SMALLER?

When you look at two objects, it's easy to tell which is bigger and which is smaller—isn't it?

Well, no! Estimating sizes can be horribly hard for the human brain.

TITCHENER ILLUSION

In this famous, very simple illusion, you see two flower shapes, each with a dot in the middle. Which of these middle dots is bigger?

To your brain, the yellow circle below probably looks bigger. But they are both actually the exact same size.

How Does It Work?

If you want to know exactly how big something is, you can measure it. But our brains don't come with an accurate tape measure installed. Instead, when we look at things, we make an instant guess about their size based on clues from the surroundings. When something is surrounded by smaller objects, it looks bigger—and vice versa.

Titchener illusion

Brain-Boggling!

Even when you can actually see the two matching dots fairly close together, your brain can't ignore the confusing "clues" telling it one is smaller and one is bigger!

HOW BIG IS THAT FACE?

The Titchener illusion is even more effective when it's made up of human faces. We're used to seeing humans of different sizes all the time, so our brains respond even more strongly to the clues.

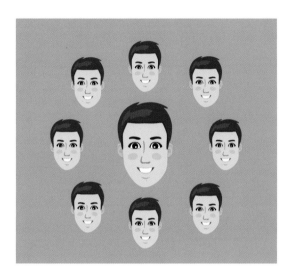

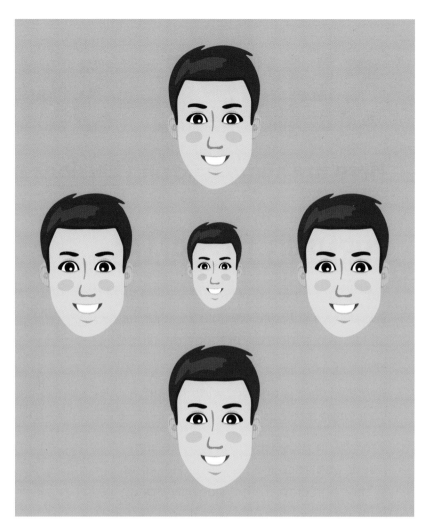

DINNER PLATES

This version of the illusion made up of dots and circles is even simpler, yet it can still trick your brain!

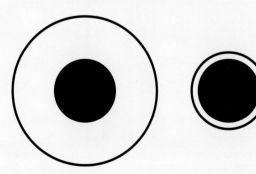

In real life, this illusion plays a part when we eat. If your meal is on a big plate and doesn't fill it up, you feel as if you're having less food. If you use a smaller plate with the same amount of food, it seems like more!

SHAPE-SHIFTERS

Here are some amazing illusions that will blow your mind!

TURNING THE TABLES

Yes, it's just a picture of two tables. But would you believe it if someone told you that the two tabletops are identical in shape and size?

"But one is a long, skinny table, and the other is a short, wide table!" your brain protests.

Wrong! To prove it, take some tracing paper and trace the outline of the "long, skinny" tabletop. Turn it sideways, and it fits on top of the other one!

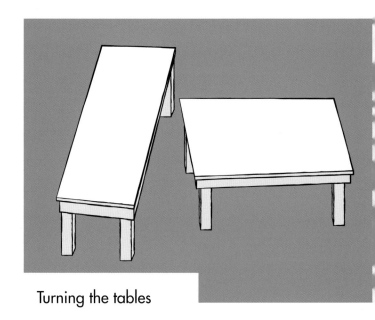

Turning the tables

How Does It Work?

This illusion is all about the way things disappear into the distance. Your brain knows that if something is stretching away from you, it's probably longer than it looks—like a road leading toward the horizon, for example.

To your eye, the road you're seeing doesn't look that long. But from experience, your brain knows it's much longer.

So when it sees something that seems to stretch away from you, your brain adds extra length in that direction. That makes one table seem longer, while the other seems wider.

SHAPE SHUFFLE

Here are some more shifty shapes. This time, it's the way they're arranged that causes all the confusion.

Are these shapes the same as each other? ▶

What about these train-track pieces? ▼

Shape shuffle

And are these two towers leaning over at the same angle? ▼

Brain-Boggling!

In these illusions, your brain is using lines and angles as clues.

The inner curve of the train track is smaller than the outer curve it is next to—so, the brain decides that the two pieces are different.

The first tower is leaning at a slight space from the vertical. But the angle between the two towers is bigger. So your brain thinks that the second tower is leaning over more.

THE LONG AND SHORT OF IT

Think you know how long a line is? Think again!

Look at this man's old-fashioned top hat, and try to decide whether it's taller than it is wide or wider than it is tall.

The top hat illusion

If you think it looks taller, most people would agree with you. As we all know, top hats are pretty tall compared to most hats! But we always tend to underestimate how wide things are compared to how tall they are. In fact, the hat's height and its width across the brim are the same.

How Does It Work?

This is called the top hat illusion, also known as the "T" illusion or the vertical/horizontal illusion. It applies to many different hats and other shapes—even a simple letter T. In all of these pictures, the height and width are the same, but most people see them as taller than they are wide.

The weird thing is, no one is really sure why our brains do this!

Test Your Sketching Skills

Try this simple test. Sketch a square on some paper, making it as square-looking as you can. Done?

Now measure your square with a ruler. If you're like most people, you'll find that you have overestimated the height and made your square shorter than it is wide!

LINE LENGTHS

This type of illusion also confuses your sense of length.

Are the two lines in this illusion the same length? ▶

They are, but the other lines seem to "pull" at them, making them seem shorter or longer to your poor, baffled brain.

What about this one? Do the two blue lines match? ▼

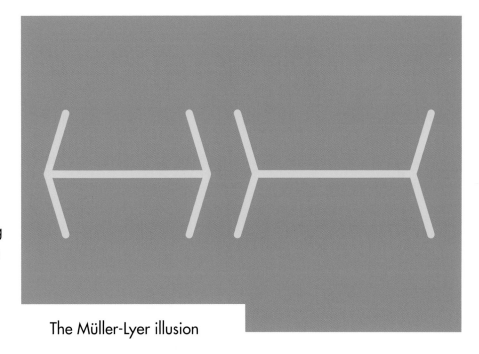

The Müller-Lyer illusion

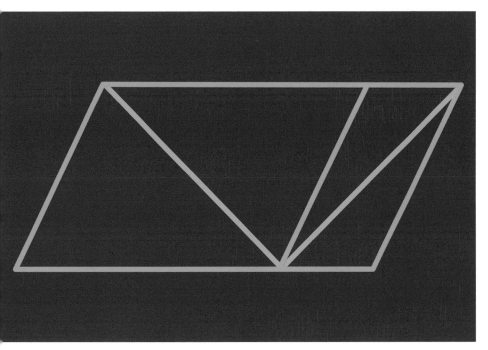

They do, but your brain is fooled by the boxes around them. One box has a smaller area, so your brain thinks the line across it must be shorter.

STRAIGHT STREET

In this picture, which blue line is longer? Of course, they're the same—but your brain knows that if this were a real street, the line on the right would be a shorter distance, so that's what it decides to see. ▼

IN PERSPECTIVE

If you see a tiny little elephant walking across your field of vision, there are two possibilities:

1. There's a tiny, little elephant floating in front of you.
2. It's a normal-size elephant, but it's far away.

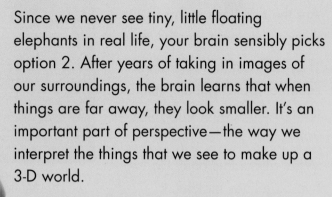

Since we never see tiny, little floating elephants in real life, your brain sensibly picks option 2. After years of taking in images of our surroundings, the brain learns that when things are far away, they look smaller. It's an important part of perspective—the way we interpret the things that we see to make up a 3-D world.

However, this effect can also cause some powerful optical illusions.

PONZO ILLUSION

Look at the two green lines in this picture. Which is longer? ▶

They're the same, but the one on the right looks much longer—and wider, too!

Below is another example of the Ponzo illusion. The pink elephants are the same size as each other—but they look totally different! ▼

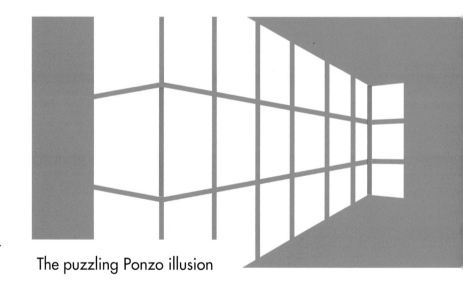

The puzzling Ponzo illusion

How Does It Work?

The diagonal lines in the background of the picture to the left tell the brain it's looking at a wall, road, or path that's stretching away at an angle. That makes the object on the left appear farther away. If it's farther away, the brain expects it to look smaller. Since it's not smaller, the brain decides it must be huge!

CRAZY CARS

This photo works even better because you're seeing a real road and real cars. The cars have been duplicated and are all the same size. However, the car that is farthest away looks huge!

PERSPECTIVE PATH

You also use your sense of perspective to guess distances. Try this!

In this picture, which letter is halfway between point A and point B? ▶

It's actually point X. Did you get it right? In real life, the distance from X to B would be much longer than the distance from X to A. This fools your brain into thinking it looks longer, too.

IN THE SHADOWS

This clever illusion looks a little bit like a Rubik's Cube ... but look more closely!

WHAT COLORS ARE THE TWO SQUARES?

Find the square in the middle of the top of the cube, then the square in the middle of the side facing you.

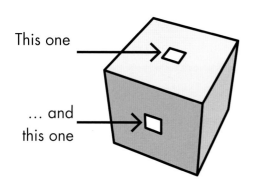

This one →

... and this one →

Though they look very different, the truth is that they are exactly the same color.

If you don't believe it, take a piece of paper, and cut two small holes in it to fit over the two squares. When you can't see the rest of the cube, it becomes clear that they really are both the same color.

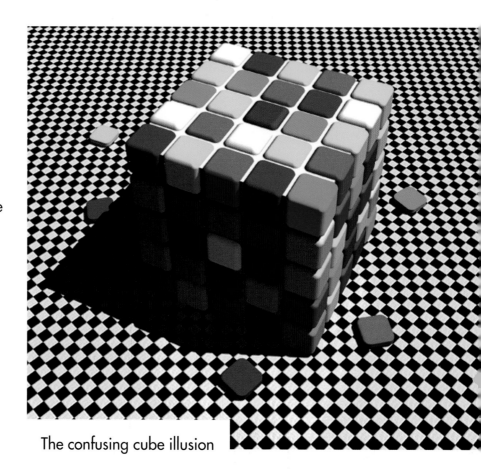

The confusing cube illusion

How Does It Work?

This modern illusion was created by brain scientist Dr. Beau Lotto in 2002. It works because of the way the brain judges colors. The top square seems to be in bright light, so you assume it's a dark color. The square on the side seems to be in shadow. But since it's actually the same color as the one on top, the brain thinks it must be a really bright color to show up so well in the dark.

SAME GRAYS

Here's a similar effect using the color gray.

You guessed it—squares A and B are the exact same shade of gray! But no matter how hard you try, they look different when you look at the whole picture and see the "shadow" falling across it.

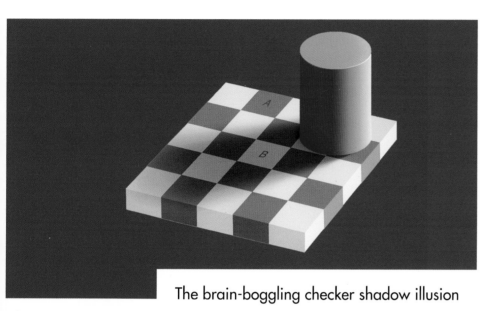

The brain-boggling checker shadow illusion

CHANGING COLORS

How can a color look like a different color? Try these illusions, and find out.

The amazing eye color illusion

Here are two pictures of a girl with gray eyes. In both pictures, both of her eyes are gray. Not only that—they're the same shade of gray. So, why do they look so different?

How Does It Work?

This illusion shows just how much the brain "adds" to whatever you're looking at. You know you're looking at a picture in a book that's made of ink on flat paper. And you know it's a cartoon, not a real person.

Yet, the bands of red and blue color still make your brain assume you're seeing a girl with red or blue light shining on one side of her face. If that happened in real life, it would color the girl's eye—for example, her eye would look reddish in the red light.

Since the eye doesn't look red (because it's actually the same shade of gray as her other eye), the brain does some amazing color math. It decides that to look that shade of gray in red light, the eye must actually be blue. So, it "sees" a blue eye. In the blue light, the effect is reversed. Genius! (But wrong.)

GROWING GREENER

Now try this crazy-colored eye-dazzler. Again, the dots here are gray, and at first, you might find they look somewhat gray, too. But keep looking. The longer you stare, the more the gray dots seem to turn greener.

Brain-Boggling!

The purple-and-red design seems to glow and overlap the spots, and your brain interprets this as a wash of reddish light. The more you stare, the more the red takes over, and the greener the dots look.

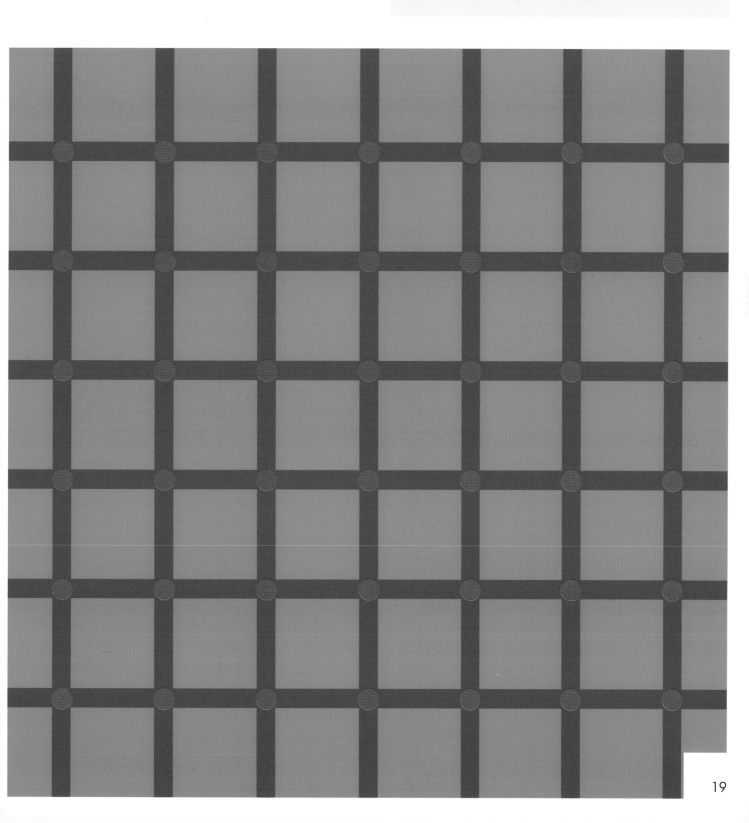

19

COLOR WEAVING

Take a good look at this picture. How many different shades of red can you see in the heart shapes?

There is actually only one red, and it's the same in all the hearts. Yet, it looks as if you can see two very different shades, because of the different colors interleaved with the red. This type of color illusion is called the Munker illusion.

SHADES OF GRAY

Here's a similar illusion that only uses black, white, and gray. It's called White's illusion. The two shades of gray are identical. ▼

The mind-boggling Munker illusion

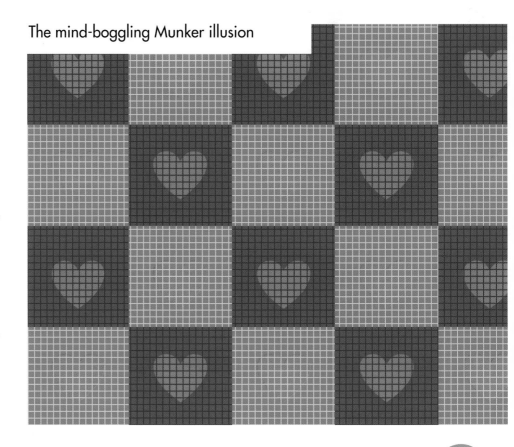

How Does It Work?

Scientists aren't sure how these illusions work! One theory is called "belongingness." If one part of an image seems to "belong" to another, it will seem to be more influenced by that part. In White's illusion, the gray blocks seem to "belong" to the horizontal stripes they are part of. So we see the gray in contrast with the black or white in the stripes, and this affects whether we see it as a darker or lighter shade.

Here's another one! In each of these pictures, the dot in the middle, and the two circles of the same color, are all the exact same shade. ▲

DO IT YOURSELF

Take a good look at how these illusions are designed, and you could try making your own with colored cards. Start with the color you want to "change," such as a bright red or green. Then interleave it with other colors to see how you can make it seem to change shade.

Brain-Boggling!

Color illusions like this aren't just interesting—they can also play a part in everyday life. People who design patterns for wallpaper or fabrics can find that they suddenly look totally wrong when placed next to another color. For designers, combining colors well is an important skill. They need to avoid unwanted illusions!

MIXED-UP MEANINGS

It's time for your brain to take a high-speed test. Are you ready?

Look at the box to the right, and say out loud the color that each word is written in, as fast as you can. (So, for the first word, you'd say "red" because it is written in red.) Try to ignore what the word actually says—just say what color it is.

How did you do? Did you start to slow down or get stuck?

MY BRAIN HURTS!

At first, it's easy because the word "red" is written in red and so on. But when they stop matching, your brain gets mixed up. You want to look at the color and say what it is, but your brain can't help trying to read the word at the same time.

red	blue	orange	purple
orange	blue	green	red
blue	purple	green	red
orange	blue	red	green
purple	orange	red	blue
green	red	blue	purple
orange	blue	red	green
purple	orange	red	blue

How Does It Work?

A test like this can really trick the brain. But it's not because you're stupid—in fact, it's the opposite. As you grow up and learn to take in information—for example, by reading—the brain learns to work automatically at high speed. Once you get better at reading, you'll read any word you see before you even have time to think about it.

The trouble is, it's very hard to stop that from happening! So, in this test, your brain is being bombarded with two different pieces of information about each word. It has to stop and figure out which is which, and that slows it down.

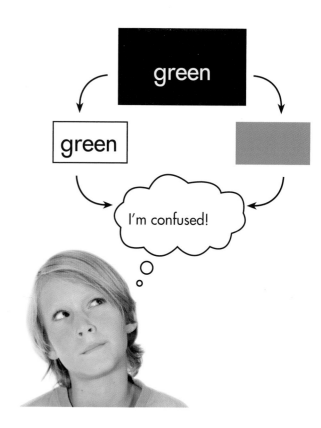

green

green

I'm confused!

SPOT THE SHAPES

It doesn't just work with colors—try this shape test, too. Normally, you can quickly identify a shape. But adding the wrong words to a set of shapes will probably make the task a lot slower.

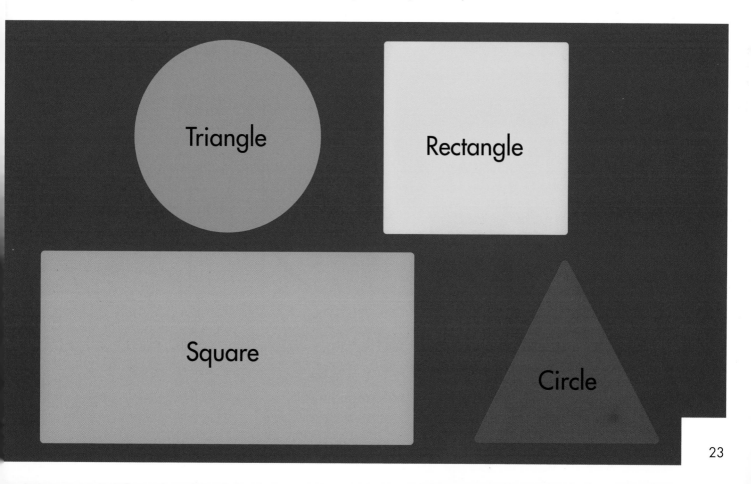

Triangle

Rectangle

Square

Circle

BROKEN BARS

Illusions don't come much simpler than this—a diagonal stick passing behind what looks like a solid bar or column. It's called the Poggendorff illusion.

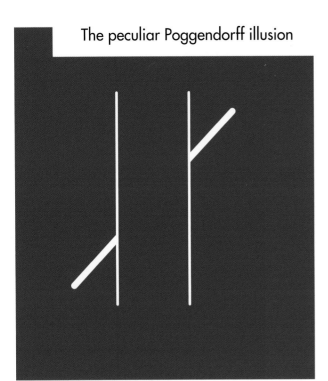

The peculiar Poggendorff illusion

The weird part is that the stick doesn't look straight. It looks as if it must have a bend in it, behind the bar. But when the stick is revealed, you can see that it is straight.

How Does It Work?

To figure out how the Poggendorff illusion works, scientists have tried removing different parts of the image and changing the position of the stick. It doesn't work if the stick is at right angles to the bar, for example. It's all to do with the angle of the diagonal line.

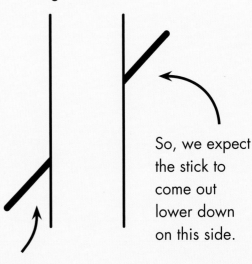

So, we expect the stick to come out lower down on this side.

The brain sees this angle as bigger than it really is.

MULTI POGGENDORFF

If you make a pattern with lots of diagonal lines and lots of bars, the effect is even stronger. It should look nice and neat, but it actually looks messy, since the lines seem to be all over the place! Are they really straight? Test them with a ruler.

POGGENDORFF ARCH

You can sometimes see Poggendorff illusions in everyday objects and buildings, such as this window arch. With a bar or pillar in the way, it looks as if the sides of the arch won't meet up.

Poggendorff Test

Try this test on a friend or family member. Draw a picture like this, with only one end of the diagonal stick showing. Then ask them to draw the line coming out of the other side of the bar, where they think it should be. Check with a ruler to see how close they were!

TWO HALVES

What does this picture show? It looks like two cushions or keyboard keys, one dark and one light. Or are they? Put a ruler (NOT a see-through one!) over the seam between the two halves, and suddenly, it's all the same shade of gray!

How Does It Work?

Sometimes called the sofa illusion, this brainteaser works in two ways. First, it uses light and shade like the shadow illusions on page 16. The upper cushion appears to be in bright sunlight, so you assume its gray surface must be dark. The lower cushion is in shadow, so you see the same gray as white with a shadow on it.

The strange "sofa" illusion

ON THE EDGE

However, this illusion also works because we judge colors and shades by comparing them to each other. This is easiest to do at the edges, where two surfaces meet. In this picture, there's a strong contrast between light and dark where the cushions meet. Your brain takes that as a clue about each entire surface.

CORNSWEET ILLUSION

You can also see this effect in the super-simple Cornsweet illusion to the right. It features two gray rectangles, both the same size. One looks paler than the other ... but is it?

In fact, the two rectangles are only different shades right in the middle, next to the dividing line. Put your finger over the line, and the difference between them disappears.

GRAY DOUGHNUTS

In this illusion, the gray circle looks two different shades when the pencil is there but not when it's taken away.

Brain-Boggling!

Why can't your brain get these things right? It's simply because it has so much information to take in. It can't look carefully at everything you see. Instead, it uses shortcuts to help it jump to conclusions. This saves time and energy for other things, such as making decisions and solving problems.

It does mean that the brain can make mistakes, but it's actually a sensible strategy!

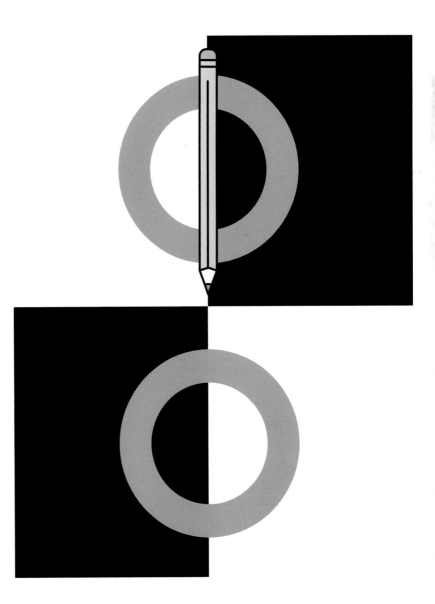

MAGIC SHADOWS

What secret creatures are hiding in the shadows?

If you visit the Mayan temple at Chichén Itzá, Mexico, at exactly the right time, you'll see a shadow serpent. At the spring and fall equinoxes (when the hours of light and darkness are exactly the same), the corner of the temple casts a wavy shadow to make the shape of a snake move down the side of the stone staircase. At the bottom, it connects to a huge carved stone snake head!

How Does It Work?

Shadows can be made to look like all kinds of shapes, depending on the angle and direction that the light is coming from. The seasons change as Earth moves around the sun, and its light hits us from different directions.

The Maya built the temple so that the snake shadow would form perfectly just twice a year. It's a kind of shadow calendar!

BLACK CAT

This shadow artwork by sculptor Larry Kagan is also very clever. The jumble of bent wires casts a shadow in a perfect cat shape when the light is accurately aimed and lit.

When you look at the artwork from in front, the wires look spread out and completely unlike the cat shape. But from the exact angle that the light is shining from, they are bunched together and carefully positioned to cast a cat-shaped shadow.

Brain-Boggling!

Imagine how tricky it would be to make a sculpture like this! To do it, the artist has to work with the light shining, so that they can see the shadow cast by each piece they add to the artwork. Then they tweak or adjust it until it builds up the image they want.

HAND SHADOWS

You can do a simple version of this with your hands—try these shadow shapes!

Black Cat by Larry Kagan

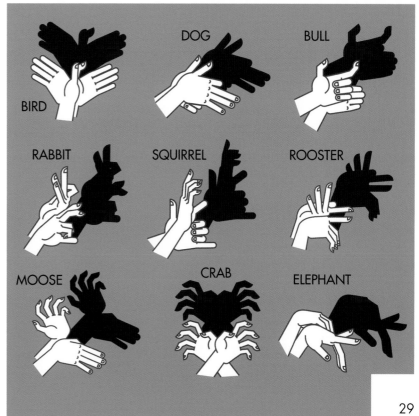

BIRD

DOG

BULL

RABBIT

SQUIRREL

ROOSTER

MOOSE

CRAB

ELEPHANT

GLOSSARY

3-D Three-dimensional, which means having length, width, and depth.

cells The tiny units that make up living things. Light-detecting cells are found in the retina.

concentric circles A series of circles of different sizes, which all have their centers at the same point.

field of vision The area of the outside world that a person can see as they look in a particular direction.

horizontal Stretching from side to side, parallel to the horizon.

illusion An image that confuses the viewer and makes them see something that is different from reality.

optical To do with light, and the way our eyes detect it.

optic nerve A bundle of nerve fibers connecting the light-sensing cells in the retina to the part of the brain that makes sense of images.

perspective The way three-dimensional objects or scenes can be shown on a flat surface, or understood by the brain from the shapes and patterns we see in real life.

retina An area of light-detecting cells at the back of the eyeball that sense patterns of light entering the eye.

vertical Stretching straight up and down, at right angles to the horizon.

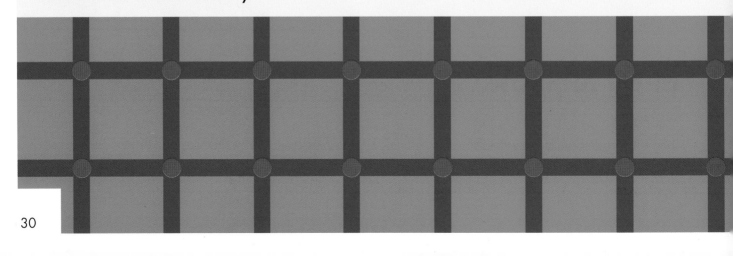

FURTHER INFORMATION

BOOKS

Gifford, Clive. *Brain Twisters: The Science of Thinking and Feeling.* Brighton, UK: Ivy Press, 2015.

Hanson, Anders, and Elissa Mann. *Cool Optical Illusions: Creative Activities That Make Math & Science Fun for Kids!* Minneapolis, MN: ABDO Publishing Company, 2014.

Sarcone, Gianni A., and Marie-Jo Waeber. *Optical Illusions: An Eye-Popping Extravaganza of Visual Tricks.* Mineola, NY: Dover Publications, 2014.

WEBSITES

nei.nih.gov/kids/optical_illusions
This National Eye Institute page has information on optical illusions and a video to watch.

www.optics4kids.org/illusions
This web page explores 17 optical illusions with a quiz.

Publisher's note to educators and parents: Our editors have carefully reviewed these websites to ensure that they are suitable for students. Many websites change frequently, however, and we cannot guarantee that a site's future contents will continue to meet our high standards of quality and educational value. Be advised that students should be closely supervised whenever they access the Internet.

INDEX